ESSENTIAL LIBRARY OF
THE US MILITARY
★ # THE US ★
NATIONAL
GUARD

Essential Library

An Imprint of Abdo Publishing | www.abdopublishing.com

ESSENTIAL LIBRARY OF
THE US MILITARY
★ **THE US** ★
NATIONAL
GUARD

BY MARCIA AMIDON LUSTED

CONTENT CONSULTANT
PROFESSOR MITCHELL YOCKELSON
DEPARTMENT OF HISTORY
UNITED STATES NAVAL ACADEMY

www.abdopublishing.com

Published by Abdo Publishing, a division of ABDO, PO Box 398166, Minneapolis,
Minnesota 55439. Copyright © 2015 by Abdo Consulting Group, Inc. International
copyrights reserved in all countries. No part of this book may be reproduced in
any form without written permission from the publisher. Essential Library™ is a
trademark and logo of Abdo Publishing.

Printed in the United States of America, North Mankato, Minnesota
042014
092014

Cover Photo: US Army
Interior Photos: US Army, 2, 52–53, 56, 62, 83, 88–89; Peter Turnley/Corbis, 6–7;
New York State Division of Military & Naval Affairs, 10; Eric Gay/AP Images, 13; US
Navy/AP Images, 14; Don Troiani/The National Guard Image Gallery, 16–17; North
Wind Picture Archives, 23; Library of Congress, 27; Donna Neary/The National Guard
Image Gallery, 28–29; AP Images, 36; Ric Feld/AP Images, 39; H. Charles McBarron/
The National Guard Image Gallery, 41; US Air Force, 42–43, 44, 49, 67; Shutterstock
Images, 47; Red Line Editorial, 63, 85; The Knoxville News Sentinel, Adam Lau/AP
Images, 50; Public Domain, 55, 100; Rex Features/AP Images, 59; Federal Emergency
Management Agency, 60–61; US Air National Guard, 70–71; Georgia Army National
Guard, 75; Virginia National Guard Public Affairs, 76, 96; The National Guard, 78–79,
90; US Army Africa, 84; Jeff Roberson/AP Images, 92

Editor: Blythe Hurley
Series Designer: Jake Nordby

Library of Congress Control Number: 2014932856

Cataloging-in-Publication Data

Lusted, Marcia Amidon.
 The US National Guard / Marcia Amidon Lusted.
  p. cm. -- (Essential library of the US military)
ISBN 978-1-62403-436-7
1. United States. National Guard--Juvenile literature.   I. Title.
355.370973--dc23

2014932856

CONTENTS

CHAPTER ONE
AT GROUND ZERO

I t was September 11, 2001, and Joseph Ranauro was at work in his civilian job as a court officer and guard in Manhattan, New York City. But Ranauro was also a sergeant in the National Guard, First Battalion, 101st Cavalry, based in Staten Island, New York. Little did he

know he would soon be called on to put his training as a guardsman to the test.

Ranauro was patrolling outside a courthouse when he heard the sound of a plane passing far too low overhead. Moments later he saw the plane slam into the side of one of the towers of the World Trade Center. Ranauro and his men responded immediately:

> *Right after we saw the plane come in, my detail gathered up all our guys, which was a detail of ten men, ten officers, most paramedics and EMTs, we got all our equipment, our oxygen bottles, our trauma bags and everything else, threw them in the van and headed toward the World Trade Center.*[1]

Ranauro and his men were helping people move away from the building when a second plane struck the other World Trade Center tower. Debris began falling all around them. Billowing clouds of dust made breathing difficult. People were falling and jumping from windows, some even landing on early responders, killing several of them.

Ranauro and several other men from his unit helped bring injured people out of the building before it collapsed. Other National Guard members who happened to be in the area joined them even though they were not deployed at the time.

Although he faced great danger, Ranauro's friend Tommy Jergens went back into the building to help bring out more injured people. Ranauro told him not to go back in, but Jergens wanted to help. Said Ranauro, "And his last words to me . . . he says, 'Joe, there's people down needing help, plus we're all paramedics.' He was a combat medic. He was assigned to the Sixty-Ninth Infantry with the New

York National Guard."[2] Jergens did not make it out of the building before it collapsed, and he died.

Ranauro was one of many off-duty National Guard members who gathered at Ground Zero that day to help however they could. They used their military training to evacuate people from the World Trade Center and to treat the injured.

Later that day, the governor of New York, George Pataki, activated most of the National Guard units in the New York City area. Many would work right at Ground Zero, digging for survivors and bodies. Others would work in a makeshift morgue set up at One Liberty Plaza. Ranauro's unit provided security in the area. Some 8,000 National Guard members eventually supported response and recovery efforts in New York City after September 11.[3]

The National Guard provided valuable services to both civilians and safety personnel immediately following the attacks of September 11, 2001, and during the aftermath.

The New York National Guard provided security at Ground Zero in the days following September 11, 2001, as part of the guard's rescue, response, and recovery efforts in lower Manhattan.

Many of them showed up to help before their units were even activated, and many would remain there for weeks. They were fulfilling one of the most basic roles of the guard, which is to help their fellow Americans during a military attack on this country.

DEALING WITH DISASTER

Flash forward to August 2005. The National Hurricane Center had just upgraded tropical storm Katrina to a hurricane. This deadly storm soon made landfall in Florida. Florida's governor, Jeb Bush, immediately declared a state of emergency. He then activated the Florida National Guard. Eight hundred National Guard members went on duty. Some prepared special vehicles to be used in areas with high water and flooding. Others assembled emergency equipment and relief supplies.

As Katrina was upgraded to a Category 2 hurricane, the neighboring states of Mississippi and Louisiana began preparing as well. Mississippi governor Haley Barbour and Louisiana governor Kathleen Blanco activated their National Guard units.

By August 29, Hurricane Katrina had become a Category 5 storm with winds of more than 170 miles per hour (274 kmh). Mississippi and Louisiana were devastated, including the city of New Orleans. Shortly after the storm passed, 30,000 more National Guard troops were on their way to the Gulf Coast area to provide search and rescue services, medical treatment,

THE SAFFIR-SIMPSON HURRICANE WIND SCALE

The National Oceanic and Atmospheric Administration (NOAA) has developed the Saffir-Simpson Hurricane Wind Scale to rate the destructiveness of hurricanes. This scale rates storms on a scale of 1 to 5, with 1 being the mildest. These storms have winds of 74 to 95 miles per hour (119 to 153 kmh) and cause only relatively minor damage. Category 5 storms are the most severe, with winds greater than 155 miles per hour (249 kmh). Category 5 storms generally cause severe damage and destruction. Katrina was a Category 5 storm, one of the five deadliest hurricanes in US history.[5]

evacuation assistance, and security.[6] These servicemen and servicewomen found themselves in difficult circumstances, without power and with few means of communication. It was almost impossible to travel in the area because of the severe flooding.

Thousands of New Orleans residents who had not been able to evacuate had taken shelter in the Superdome, an arena that is home to the National Football League's New Orleans Saints. Two hundred Louisiana National Guard members were providing medical care, food, and other services there. A similar scenario was taking place at the New Orleans Convention Center. There were rumors of violence, poor sanitary conditions, and untimely deaths at both locations. One thousand guard members were called

SOLDIER'S CREED

The men and women in the National Guard follow the same creed as other US Army soldiers. This creed expresses their mission and their feelings about being in the guard.

Soldier's Creed
  I am an American Soldier.
  I am a warrior and a member
    of a team. I serve the people
    of the United States, and live
    the Army Values.
  I will always place the
    mission first.
  I will never accept defeat.
  I will never quit.

I will never leave a
    fallen comrade.
I am disciplined, physically and
    mentally tough, trained and
    proficient in my warrior tasks
    and drills.
I always maintain my arms, my
    equipment and myself.
I am an expert and I am
    a professional.
I stand ready to deploy,
    engage, and destroy the
    enemies of the United States
    of America in close combat.
I am a guardian of freedom
    and the American way of life.
I am an American Soldier.[7]

The National Guard arrived in the area of the New Orleans Convention Center, where residents had been waiting for days to be evacuated after Hurricane Katrina.

in to help deal with the situation. According to US Army lieutenant colonel Jacques Thibodeaux, "Our job was to come in and conduct a rescue mission, to provide law and order, provide relief, and then to evacuate the facility."[8] But despite the rumors, when the troops entered the center in full riot gear, they were surprised to be greeted like heroes. In only 30 minutes, they had the situation under control with no violence at all.

By the end of September, the National Guard units activated to deal with the aftermath of Hurricane Katrina had flown more than 10,200 missions, airlifted more than 88,000 people to safety, moved more than 18,000 short tons (16,300 metric tons) of emergency and relief supplies, and saved at least 17,000 lives.[9]

"The Guard did what the Guard does best," said US Army lieutenant general H. Steven Blum. "It answered the call, it saw the need, it prepared so that when it was needed, it was ready and it was there." Blum said he has strong feelings about the guard's response to Katrina, which was the largest relief operation in US history. "If I sound a little proud about the Guard, I am," he said. "I couldn't be more proud."[10]

IN WAR AND IN PEACE

The National Guard's responses to these two disasters, one natural and the other an act of terrorism, demonstrate how the guard has evolved from its long-ago beginnings as a volunteer civilian force, or militia, during America's colonial times. Today's National Guard has two missions.

A National Guard multipurpose utility truck brings supplies to the Superdome in downtown New Orleans after Hurricane Katrina.

One part of its duty lies in homeland defense. This includes active military and war duty, increasingly overseas. But the guard also performs homeland security missions here in the United States. This means dealing with the aftermath of disasters and providing security in situations such as riots and violent protests.

Most important, the men and women who perform these missions already have regular civilian jobs or are attending school. Yet they must be ready to leave at a moment's notice to go where they are needed when their unit is activated. While the National Guard's roots go back to the founding of the United States, the guard still represents a group of ordinary US citizens dedicated to serving their country and providing a strong and ready resource to serve their fellow citizens.

CHAPTER TWO

MINUTEMEN TO MILITIA

The idea behind the National Guard is the same as that of other militias throughout history: to maintain a group of regular citizens who are trained and can serve as soldiers in the event their country needs them, either for defense or for aid. This is the origin of the term *citizen soldier*. Soldiers of the National Guard are regular citizens

who can become soldiers when necessary, but who are not part of the regular standing army. American militias go back to the time before the United States was a nation, when Americans were first settling the country and then when they began struggling against British rule.

DEFENDING A WILDERNESS

The first American citizen soldiers were actually British colonists. When the first British settlers founded the Jamestown settlement in Virginia in 1607, they knew their survival depended on being able to defend themselves against hostile Native American tribes, as well as other European explorers. They formed a citizen soldier defense based on the British militia system. These men trained in military techniques, built defensive walls and a fort, carried weapons, and took turns as watchmen. But they were not full-time soldiers.

When the Pilgrims landed in Plymouth during 1620 in what would later become the state of Massachusetts, they brought with them Captain Myles Standish as their military adviser. After the Pilgrims' arrival, Standish quickly established a Plymouth militia. When the Puritans arrived in Massachusetts Bay Colony in 1630 and began building settlements, they created companies of militia as well.

On December 13, 1636, the colony of Massachusetts's General Court required the

A THANKSGIVING DRILL

Not only did the Pilgrims establish their own militia for the purposes of maintaining watchmen, guards, and alarms, but this force even played a role in the first Thanksgiving celebration. In 1621, the Pilgrims conducted a militia muster as part of that first Thanksgiving. A muster is a formal gathering of troops for inspection, display, or exercise.

establishment of the first official militia regiments in North America. Because the Massachusetts Colony was the first government body in what would eventually become the United States to officially create military regiments, December 13, 1636, is recognized as the official birthday of the National Guard.

Various militia groups defended the American settlements and colonies through two wars with Native Americans, the Pequot War of 1637 and King Philip's War in 1675. Motivated by these and other events, Connecticut, Rhode Island, and New Hampshire also formed militia companies that could be ready at short notice to defend their settlements.

Massachusetts took the idea of instant readiness even further. In 1645, legislators there passed a law requiring each militia company to choose a third of its members who would "respond to alarms within thirty minutes."[1] This was an example of a type of militia known as minutemen, so named because they could supposedly be ready at only a minute's notice to protect their homes and towns.

Colonial militias participated in the French and Indian War from 1754 to 1763. First US president George Washington himself even served in one of these units. These men fought alongside the British, who wanted to maintain their dominance in the New World. However, interactions between the Colonial militias and the British army during this time eventually became part of a souring relationship between Colonial settlers and the British government. British military commanders considered the American colonists to be poor, undisciplined soldiers and often relegated them to support roles. The colonists began to resent this treatment, and they increasingly saw the British as repressive and threatening. This discontent, among others, would grow until the eruption of the American Revolution.

REVOLUTIONARY TIMES

The Revolutionary War (1775–1783) started with a standoff between Colonial minutemen and British soldiers called regulars at Lexington and Concord in Massachusetts on April 19, 1775. Historians often refer to these two battles as "the shot heard 'round the world."[2]

Leaders within the Colonial militia knew British general Thomas Gage was planning a raid to capture supplies of gunpowder

A FREE CITIZEN

In 1758, a document called the "Exercise for the Militia of the Province of the Massachusetts-Bay" was published by order of the captain general of that colony. It was essentially an instruction manual meant to educate the men who joined the militia about organization and fighting. Part of the document has become a famous quote concerning the reasons why regular citizens should join the militia:

Every Man therefore that wishes to secure his own Freedom, and thinks it his Duty to defend that of his Country, should, as he prides himself on being a Free Citizen, think it his truest Honour to be a Soldier Citizen.[3]

at Concord. His superiors in London, England, considered the Colonial militias to be simply "a rude Rabble without plan, without concert and without conduct."[4] Little did they know the colonies had taken the minuteman concept to heart. Colonial leaders had found volunteers who could be instantly ready and supplied these men with two weeks' worth of food and ammunition, as well as instituting a strict schedule of drills and training.

The Colonial militias also had better military intelligence than the British realized. On the night of April 18, they knew Gage's raid was forthcoming. They were ready to send out a warning using lanterns hung in the steeple of Boston's Old North Church. One lantern would mean the British army would march over land, while two would mean the troops were taking boats across the Charles River. This was the famous "one if by land, two if by sea" message. That same night, Paul Revere, along with several others, made his famous ride to Lexington, warning people along the way the British army was coming.

On April 19, the British met with a company of minutemen and militia on the town green in Lexington. These forces met again at the North Bridge in Concord. The militia was able to defeat the British and pursue them back to Boston. The Colonial militia forces inflicted heavy losses on the well-trained British soldiers, known as redcoats. As General Gage reported after his defeat, "Whoever looks upon [the colonials] as an irregular mob, will find himself very much mistaken. They have men amongst them who know very well what they are about."[5]

A REGULAR ARMY

The value of the citizen soldiers fighting in the militia was seen time and again during the Revolutionary War. At the Battle of Bunker Hill, the militia fought against a force of 2,400 British troops, severely weakening one of the best professional armies in the world.[6] Bunker Hill became a symbol of the militia's fighting spirit. However, it also showed the need for a more permanent standing army to fight what was becoming a larger war.

On June 14, the colonists' political body, the Continental Congress, created the Continental army. This new force was placed under the command of George Washington. In addition to maintaining their militias, the colonies would now be required to raise, equip, and train regiments for the Continental army. The Continental army and the militiamen would continue to fight together throughout the Revolutionary War. The militias provided

A REVOLUTIONARY MYTH

Most Americans were taught in their US history classes that during his famous midnight ride, Paul Revere shouted, "The British are coming!" But this is a myth. What Revere actually called out during his ride was "The Regulars are coming out!"[7] This was a more specific warning that the British army, fully trained and one of the strongest fighting forces in the world, was on its way.

extra manpower when needed. They also attacked parties of redcoats foraging for supplies, monitored enemy troop movements, suppressed the continuing uprisings of Native Americans, fought against British naval raids, enforced local laws, and guarded prisoners of war.

After the end of the Revolutionary War, militias continued in several states on a volunteer basis. During his presidency, Thomas Jefferson created defense plans for the country that included a strong navy, a regular standing army, and the continued use of a militia. It would be the militia's job to contain hostile forces in the event of an enemy invasion until regular army troops could arrive.

Paul Revere's famous midnight ride warned the minutemen of Lexington to prepare to do battle with the British regulars.

Then the two forces would work together to defeat any invaders. Jefferson's military policy mandated "a well-disciplined militia—our best reliance in peace and for the first months of war, till Regulars may relieve them."[8]

THE WAR OF 1812 AND AFTER

While this seemed like a sound plan, during the War of 1812 (1812–1815), the militia and the regular army did not always cooperate well. Some militia units operated independently of the regular army, while others fought alongside the regulars under army leadership. Some citizen soldiers failed to show up to fight against British

"TAKE GOOD CARE OF THE CHILDREN"

The man shown on the symbol of the National Guard is minuteman Captain Isaac Davis. This Colonial militia member from Concord, Massachusetts, left his family and picked up a musket to defend his country at the beginning of the Revolutionary War. As his wife, Hannah, recorded in her diary:

> The alarm was given early in the morning, and my husband lost no time in making ready to go to Concord with his company. My husband said but little that morning. He seemed serious and thoughtful; but never seemed to hesitate. He only said, "Take good care of the children," and was soon out

of sight. . . . In the afternoon they brought him home a corpse.[9]

Davis was a gunsmith and leader of the Acton Minute Men, one of the best trained, drilled, and equipped militias in all of Massachusetts. When asked if he was afraid to lead his men against the British forces massed at Concord's North Bridge, Davis responded, "No, I am not, and I haven't a man that is afraid to go."[10] The National Guard honors this minuteman, who represents so well the spirit of those who may be called on to protect their country at a moment's notice, on its official logo.

raiding parties. Other militia groups with strong leaders did fight hard in some battles. They helped defend the city of Baltimore, Maryland, when the British landed there. And a garrison of troops and militia working together successfully defended Fort McHenry when it was bombed by British ships. This is the event that inspired Francis Scott Key to write the song that would eventually become the national anthem of the United States, "The Star-Spangled Banner."

After the end of the War of 1812 and during the decades that followed, interest in the enrolled militia—the term used to describe militia groups that enrolled volunteers rather than using a draft system requiring people to join—began to decrease. Many states abolished mandatory militia service during the 1840s. The militia system was in danger of simply fading away.

STRUGGLES IN THE SOUTHWEST

During the mid-1800s, voluntary military forces proved essential to the safety and stability of a still-young nation. The militia of the Republic of Texas was responsible for gaining Texas's independence from Mexico by fighting at San Jacinto and the Alamo in 1836.

Militia units also contributed to the success of the United States in defeating Mexico in the Mexican-American War (1846–1848) and gaining territory that would later become the states of California, New Mexico, Arizona, Nevada, Colorado, and Utah. President James Polk relied heavily on volunteer regiments during this conflict. A total of 116,000 soldiers, from both militias and the regular army, fought in Mexico. Of that group, 75 percent were militiamen.[11]

THE CIVIL WAR

As tensions grew in the United States before the Civil War (1861–1865), new militia groups sprang up all over the country in response to the need for preparedness. Militias would play an important role during this bloody conflict. In the South, militia groups were the main force available to the Confederate government for seizing federal forts and other facilities. States that still had enrolled militia companies called those men up for service. This was particularly true for Northern militias. These troops would both guard and defend the nation's capital and fight against the Confederates.

Both enrolled and volunteer militia companies made up a large number of the troops that fought on both sides during the Civil War. President Abraham Lincoln called up 75,000 militiamen to serve on the Union side, and the South had approximately 33,000.[12] One of these militia companies, the Seventh New York Regiment, was among the first known groups to adopt the title "National Guard" and use that name on their equipment and uniforms.

CHANGES IN TIMES OF PEACE

Ten years after the end of the Civil War, interest in volunteer militia groups was on the rise once again. The militia would prove useful during the Great Railroad Strike of 1877, when disgruntled workers shut down many railroads. Fifteen states called out their militiamen to curb violence and reestablish regular rail service. As a result of this strike, many states increased their military budgets to allow for the maintenance of what were now known as National Guard groups.

By 1895, the National Guard was firmly established across the United States with 115,699 members, making it four times larger than the regular army.[13]

Several members of the Twenty-Second New York State Militia—among the 75,000 militiamen to serve during the Civil War—gathered near Harpers Ferry, Virginia, in 1861.

CHAPTER THREE
WORLD WARS AND BEYOND

By the turn of the century, the United States had increased the size of its regular army. But in 1903, Congress was unwilling to spend the money to add even more soldiers to the nation's military forces. Politicians at that time felt maintaining a larger army would be

The training the Second Connecticut Infantry received when it was called up after Pancho Villa's 1916 border raid would serve its members well when they were mobilized again to join the fight in World War I.

too expensive. They also feared having a large standing military would create a warlike culture that was not in keeping with the way the United States saw itself at that time.

THE MILITIA ACT OF 1903

As the 1800s ended and the 1900s began, the military needs of the nation grew. Government decision makers recalled how effectively the militia had served the country in various previous conflicts. Many people felt maintaining strong militias could be an effective, low-cost alternative to creating a larger standing army. Reserve forces would still meet the needs of their own individual states. But if these men were properly trained and equipped, they could also serve as an indispensable part of the regular army when they were needed.

THE FATHER OF THE MODERN GUARD

Senator Charles W. F. Dick has often been called "the father of the modern National Guard" because of his strong support for the Militia Act of 1903, which required guardsmen to attend drills and summer training camp. This new law also mandated that guardsmen be paid for the time they spent training. Dick also helped get federal funding for the guard and worked to solidify the relationship between the guard and the regular military. He was also able to get the support the act needed in order to move through Congress and become a law with almost no opposition.

The Militia Act of 1903 officially recognized two different classes of the militia. The organized militia (the National Guard) was placed under joint federal and state control. The second category, called the reserve militia, included all men in the United States between 18 and 45 years of age who were eligible to be drafted for military service but hadn't officially joined the National Guard. This has since been changed to include men between the ages of 18 and 25. This part of the act is why young men are still required to register with the Selective Service today when they reach the age of 18.

The result of this new appreciation for voluntary military forces and the important role they could continue to play for the nation was the Militia Act of 1903. This officially converted the volunteer militia into the National Guard. Guard units would now receive additional funding and equipment. But in return they would have to meet federal standards for training and organization.

The National Guard now had an official role in the US military. The amount of money budgeted to the guard would rise in subsequent years, reaching $4 million in 1908. The number of men enrolled in the National Guard also increased after the Militia Act of 1903, rising from 116,547 in 1903 to 132,194 by 1916.[1]

NATIONAL DEFENSE ACT OF 1916

Between a revolution in Mexico and the conflicts brewing in Europe that would soon lead to World War I (1914–1918), international tensions were on the rise early in the 1900s. In response to these threats, Congress passed the National Defense Act of 1916. This law again reorganized the standing army and called for guardsmen and reservists to be ready to fight in Europe if need be.

Meanwhile, President Woodrow Wilson had ordered regular army troops to Mexico in March 1916 to track down the Mexican revolutionary leader Francisco "Pancho" Villa. Villa had crossed the Mexican border as part of a

IN THE SKIES

The mobilization of National Guard troops to defend the US-Mexican border in 1916 marked the first time a flying guard unit was activated. Although it did not serve along the border, the New York First Aero Company mobilized and reported to Texas with regular ground guard units.

raid on the town of Columbus, New Mexico, killing 17 Americans. Wilson sent 10,000 regular soldiers, almost all of the army troops available in the Southwest at that time, to cross the Rio Grande River into Mexico to strike back.[2] As a result, states along the Mexican border (Texas, New Mexico, and Arizona) began worrying about their citizens' safety. In response, the National Guard was activated for the first time in the twentieth century.

President Wilson deployed 25,000 guardsmen from as far away as Connecticut to ensure the safety of the border states.[3] While none of these units saw active combat or entered into Mexico, they provided valuable services to the people of the Southwest. They patrolled the US-Mexican border and stood ready to help the regular army troops in Mexico if necessary. This mobilization also served as an opportunity to practice the activation of a large number of guard troops in a real-life situation. The government was able to identify areas that needed attention, such as training and equipment. Officials also recognized the importance of recruiting soldiers who met fitness standards and understood the responsibilities that were part of their enlistment.

WORLD WAR I

On April 6, 1917, America officially declared war on
Germany and entered World War I. The largest percentage
of troops initially sent to fight in Europe were actually
activated guardsmen. By August, the entire National
Guard, a total of 379,701 men, had been activated.[4] These
men received specialized training in trench warfare. Their
new infantry divisions were also designed to be more
effective for that type of fighting. Newly divided into 16
numbered divisions, guard troops were soon deployed to
the battlefields of France.

By the end of the war, 433,478 guardsmen had fought
for their country. In fact, approximately 40 percent of all
the American army troops sent to Europe during World
War I were National Guard members, as were 43 percent of
those killed or wounded (103,721 men).[5] Many guardsmen
received the Medal of Honor, including 12 members of the
Thirtieth Division, from North Carolina, South Carolina,
and Tennessee.

Despite their outstanding work in the war, the
National Guard faced a threat to its existence in 1920
in the form of a new National Defense Act. The US War
Department had devised a plan for a standing army that
could support the United States' new role as a world power.
The plan called for a standing force of approximately
500,000 troops, backed up with a reserve force of 500,000

IN THE TRENCHES

During World War I, the development of new types of explosives and artillery made it possible for armies to fire at each other more accurately over long distances. The safest way to protect troops against this type of artillery was to dig long, narrow, deep trenches in the ground. Soldiers could stand up and move around in these trenches and still be protected from enemy fire. Although these trenches were effective, conditions in them were often terrible. Soldiers endured living with mud, rats, lice, and disease.

trained reservists.[6] But the plan made no specific mention of the National Guard.

However, Congress rejected this plan and decided instead on a standing army of 280,000 soldiers to defend the United States overseas and along its borders. The National Guard was once again designated as the United States' official reserve force, with a maximum of 435,000 soldiers.[7] The guard was once again recognized as an important part of the US military.

THE GREAT DEPRESSION

America entered the Great Depression after a stunning stock market crash in 1929. The Great Depression was a severe worldwide economic depression that took place during the decade preceding World War II (1939–1945). It was the longest, most widespread, and most severe depression of the 1900s. Many Americans found themselves without jobs and faced with economic instability. But those men who were members of the

National Guard could still count on $75 a month to support their families as long as they attended drills at their local armory and went to training camp during the summer.

The National Guard played an important role in maintaining stability in the United States during this time. Guardsmen were called to maintain order during labor strikes. The California National Guard restored order after regular policemen and bystanders were killed during rioting following the San Francisco longshoremen's strike in 1934. Guardsmen were also called out to respond to a steelworkers' strike in Defiance, Ohio, in 1935. During this conflict, guard air units dropped tear gas to break up rioting crowds. In part because of the guard's importance during this time, in 1933 Congress passed an amendment to the National Defense Act of 1916. The amendment officially defined the National Guard's role as both a reserve force for the national military and a force for state governments to draw on to keep the peace at home.

WORLD WAR II AND BEYOND

As World War II began in Europe, President Franklin D. Roosevelt increased the National Guard's readiness as a reserve for the regular army. In September 1940, the first National Guard units were called up for active federal duty. The National Guard of Hawaii fired the first shots of the guard during World War II fighting the Japanese attack

National Guardsmen advanced near a town in Italy, where the Thirty-Fourth Division saw action during World War II.

on Pearl Harbor on December 17, 1941. They also fought on the beaches of Normandy, France, during the D-day invasion by Allied forces that was critical in retaking Europe from the Axis powers. National Guard units served in both the European and Pacific theaters of war, and these 300,000 men were a vital part of the Allies' victory.[8] They fought alongside—and just as hard as—regular US Army troops.

The National Guard would continue playing a vital role in US conflicts throughout the latter half of the

1900s. During the Korean War (1950–1953), almost 140,000 guardsmen were mobilized.[9] And members of the Kentucky Army National Guard were ordered to serve in the Vietnam War (1956–1975) in late 1968. One of these units lost nine men, with another 37 wounded, when North Vietnamese troops overran Fire Base Tomahawk on June 19, 1969.[10] However, there was controversy about the participation of National Guard units during the Vietnam War. President Lyndon B. Johnson had refused to mobilize guard and reserve units for this conflict. He instead decided to rely on expanding active forces and drafting soldiers from the general population.

Guardsmen were called up on several occasions to serve at both the state and federal levels during the later 1900s. The National Guard helped preserve order during civil rights riots in Los Angeles, Detroit, and Chicago. They also responded to antiwar protests during the Vietnam War, especially on college campuses. Members of the guard also served a vital role during the Persian Gulf War (1990–1991), starting

KENT STATE

One of the guard's darkest chapters took place at Kent State University on May 4, 1970. An Ohio National Guard unit had been called in to deal with an antiwar protest involving 1,000 students on the campus. According to news reports, the 28 guardsmen were surrounded by students, who began throwing rocks. There were also reports a sniper had fired at them from a nearby rooftop. The guardsmen opened fire, killing four students and wounding eight others. The Kent State incident sparked riots and protests at colleges all over the country.

in 1990. When President George H. W. Bush announced a buildup of US troops in Iraq after its leader, Saddam Hussein, ordered the invasion of Kuwait, approximately 65,000 National Guard troops were called to active duty to serve in Operation Desert Shield.[11] This was followed by Operation Desert Storm in January 1991, which ended six weeks later.

The National Guard entered the 2000s still carrying out its role as an important reserve force for both domestic peacekeeping and international defense. The dawning of the new century would add a new dimension to its role when terrorism hit close to home.

INTEGRATING THE GUARD

African-American men have served in US militia units since the birth of the United States. But they almost always served in racially segregated units.

CAPTURING SADDAM

After the US-led invasion of Iraq in 2003, former Iraqi president Saddam Hussein stayed in hiding for several months. A group of nurses serving with the 193rd Special Operations wing of the Air National Guard from Pennsylvania played a major role in his capture in December 2003. These women were working at a medical facility in Kirkuk, Iraq, treating civilians. The families of the people who received care from these seven nurses were very grateful. In return, they provided information about where Hussein might be hiding. This knowledge was combined with other sources of intelligence, resulting in the capture of Hussein. The "Kirkuk Seven," as the nurses later came to be known, were honored for their role in Hussein's capture by Pennsylvania governor Edward G. Rendell.

Guardsmen from the 265th Quartermaster Detachment served as part of Operation Desert Shield.

After the Civil War, when Congress allowed the states to form new militia units, the only criterion was that their members had to be loyal to the Union. This allowed many black militia units to form, and they were allowed to elect black officers instead of being commanded by white officers, as was the case with black units in the regular army.

THE RAINBOW DIVISION

One of the most famous National Guard divisions is known as the Rainbow Division. The group got its name because its members came from 26 different states and the District of Columbia. When marked on a map, these states looked like a rainbow-shaped arc across the country. In fact, Colonel Douglas MacArthur once said, "The Forty-Second Division stretches like a rainbow from one end of America to the other."[13] The Rainbow Division is also known for its service in two world wars. During World War I, the men of this division participated in six different campaigns. In fact, one out of every sixteen casualties was from the Rainbow Division. During World War II, the Rainbow Division was one of the first American units to enter Germany, capturing 6,000 square miles (15,540 sq km) of Nazi territory. They also helped liberate the Nazi concentration camp at Dachau.

Guard units became racially integrated in the northern US states starting in 1947. National Guard units in the southern US states did not integrate until the 1960s.

Women first began serving in the National Guard during the 1950s, when they took on roles as nurse officers. However, Congress had to pass special legislation before women could serve as active, regular members of the guard. This was accomplished during the 1970s, when many parts of the US military were expanding women's roles. By 1977, there were more than 11,000 women in the guard. Along with African Americans, women were an important source of new recruits during this time.[12]

The African-American guardsmen of the 369th Infantry came to be known as the "Hell Fighters" after their heroic service during World War I.

CHAPTER FOUR
AN EVOLVING ROLE IN WARTIME

The various militia groups in US history have always served as an aid to regular military forces when needed. But the exact nature of the relationship between the National Guard and the regular US Army has evolved

A quartet of F-16C Fighting Falcons from the 115th Fighter Wing, Wisconsin Air National Guard, flew over Wisconsin's capital city of Madison on October 18, 2008, to celebrate the unit's sixtieth anniversary.

and changed throughout the 1900s and early 2000s. Today, the guard and the army are connected in more ways than ever before.

THE AIR NATIONAL GUARD'S GROWING PAINS

One of the changes that grew out of the United States' use of the National Guard during World War II was the establishment of the Air National Guard (ANG). The air force itself was part of the army at that time, and was called the Army Air Corps. This changed when Congress passed the National Security Act of 1947. This law reorganized the armed forces, designating the air force as a separate branch of the military. That same law created the ANG as a citizen pilot group that would assist the air force in the same way the guard assists the regular army.

National Guard members flew B-24 bombers over Romania during World War II.

The ANG had a rough start. Much like the sometimes rocky relationship between the Army National Guard and the regular army, the ANG didn't have a good relationship with the air force, it had obsolete airplanes and equipment, and it had trouble recruiting pilots. The air force sometimes seemed to consider the ANG to be simply a "state-sponsored flying club."[1] But during the Korean War, when only a third of the regular National Guard was called to active duty, 80 percent of the ANG was directly involved. This involvement, amounting to 45,000 men, opened the air force's eyes to the value of the ANG.[2] The air force now understood citizen pilots needed specific missions to fly during wars, more involvement with overall air force missions, and the same training standards as regular air force active-duty squadrons.

By 1960, approximately 71,000 men belonged to ANG units.[3] The pilots of the ANG were trained in tactical fighting, reconnaissance, airlifting heavy equipment and

THE ANG v. THE ARNG

When the National Guard became two entities—an air force arm and an army arm—it became necessary to distinguish between the two. ARNG is the abbreviation used to refer to the Army National Guard, which is the branch of the guard in which traditional ground soldiers serve in army roles. The ANG is the abbreviation for the Air National Guard, which is made up of pilots and other personnel necessary to carry out and service aerial missions.

RUNWAY ALERT

In 1953, the ANG participated in a program called Runway Alert. During the Cold War, when the United States was concerned about the threat of air attack from the Soviet Union, ANG fighter squadrons went on alert at certain US airfields from one hour before daylight until one hour after sundown each day. Eventually 25 ANG squadrons were on alert around the clock at these key airfields around the country. This was one of the first instances of the air force using guard and reserve groups to support their mission.

personnel, refueling other aircraft in flight, and evacuating the wounded by air.

During the Vietnam War, ANG citizen pilots conducted medical and other support missions. Eventually some ANG units were called up to active duty in Vietnam as well. By the end of that war, the ANG and the air force were working more closely together than ever.

As with the original National Guard, the role of the ANG has expanded. It now serves as a vital component of conflicts overseas. As Michael Doubler says in *The National Guard and Reserve*:

[Afghanistan and Iraq] dramatically illustrate that citizen-soldiers are not only a vital portion of America's first line of defense but also that the country can simply not go to war without them. From the very beginning of those campaigns [they] have provided coalition forces with the full spectrum of combat and support capabilities in the air, on the ground, and at sea.[4]

AIR NATIONAL GUARD RANKS

Enlisted

Airman Basic
Airman
Airman First Class ·············>
Senior Airman
Staff Sergeant
Technical Sergeant
Master Sergeant
<············ Senior Master Sergeant
Chief Master Sergeant
Chief Master Sergeant of the Air Force

Officer

Second Lieutenant
First Lieutenant
Captain ·················>
Major
<··········· Lieutenant Colonel
Colonel
Brigadier General
Major General ·············>
Lieutenant General
General

TRANSFORMATION

After the Vietnam War, the US military shifted from a draft system, in which young men are called into military service by the government, to an all-volunteer military force. In order to ensure the United States would always have enough troops to maintain its security, the government created the Total Force Policy. This policy would make the National Guard and the ANG even more important to the country's overall military operations. This shift in policy and planning was known as transformation. According to Mary Corbett, author of *National Guard 101*:

> We began shifting from large, heavy, overlapping, and overwhelming forces to smaller, lighter, and more mobile forces that made up for their loss of size with high-technology lethality. The originators of the Total Force Policy intended that if the US military had to fight a war, the Reserve components would be an integral part of the fight.[5]

PROTECTING THE SKIES

The ANG was among the first branches of the military to respond after the terrorist attacks of September 11, 2001. Only eight minutes after the second airplane slammed into the World Trade Center, a flight of F-15 aircraft from an ANG squadron in Massachusetts appeared over lower Manhattan. And just moments after the Pentagon was hit, a group of F-16 aircraft flew over the damaged building. This gave the frightened people on the ground in both locations a sense of security. Across the country, ANG members rushed to their bases as soon as they heard the news of the attacks, offering their services.

The impact of this shift was obvious when the United States fought against Saddam Hussein during the Persian Gulf War in 1990 and 1991, and again when the United States pursued military action in Iraq and Afghanistan. Both the National Guard and the ANG played an important role in those conflicts, due in part to the changes brought about by the Total Force Policy.

Today members of the National Guard are soldiers of both their home states and the federal government. At this time, almost every guard unit in the United States has served at least one round of active duty, either at home or overseas in Iraq or Afghanistan. This had not been the case previously since World War II. The National Guard and ANG have become increasingly important as part

The 102nd Fighter Wing of the Massachusetts ANG was among the first responders to the attacks of September 11, 2001.

of the total US military force when it comes to national security both at home and in foreign countries. They have carried out the same roles and missions as regular military personnel and, in some cases, have even carried a greater load than their regular army and air force counterparts in terms of supplying manpower for overseas conflicts. But the role of international peacekeeper and defender of the United States is just one side of what the guard does for its country.

Tennessee National Guard soldiers prepared to board Kiowa helicopters leaving for Fort Hood, Texas, where they were to train for their upcoming deployment to Afghanistan.

US DEPARTMENT OF DEFENSE BUDGET
FISCAL YEAR 2014

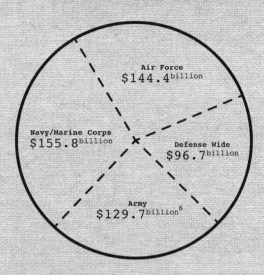

Air Force
$144.4 billion

Navy/Marine Corps
$155.8 billion

Defense Wide
$96.7 billion

Army
$129.7 billion[6]

SELECTED FISCAL YEAR 2014 EXPENDITURES,
US GOVERNMENT (IN BILLIONS OF DOLLARS)

	Army National Guard	Air National Guard
Personnel	$7.7	$3.1
Overseas Personnel	$0.2	$0.01
Operations and Maintenance	$6.8	$6.4
Overseas Operations and Maintenance	$0.1	$0.02
Equipment	$0.3	$0.3
Construction	$0.3	$0.1[7]

*The federal government covers much of the costs of the National Guard, but the states contribute some funds.

THE NATIONAL GUARD TODAY

The National Guard entered the 2000s as a defined militia force of volunteers with clear roles at both the state and national levels. It is these dual roles that make the guard so vital for both national defense and domestic peacekeeping and relief missions.

52

Members of the Florida National Guard entered a mobile home park in Melbourne, Florida, to evacuate residents after Tropical Storm Fay hit the area on August 21, 2008.

According to their particular constitution and laws, states can call out their National Guard units at any time for missions including peacekeeping or disaster relief. During these times, the governor of the state becomes the commander in chief of the guard. These missions are undertaken at the state's expense. These units can use the airplanes, vehicles, and other equipment that have been provided to them by the federal government, although they have to repay the cost of consumable supplies such as food and fuel. State governors have activated the National Guard in response to disasters such as floods, earthquakes, and wildfires, as well as to handle riots, protests, terrorist attacks, and other man-made emergencies.

Article 1, section 8 of the US Constitution authorizes the use of the National Guard "to execute the Laws of the Union, suppress Insurrections and repel Invasions."[1] Under the War Powers clause of the Constitution, the government can also mobilize guard units for national defense to serve in combat missions all over the world. This is sometimes called "federalizing" because guard members become soldiers of the federal government during these missions. When this happens, National Guard troops are under the command of the US president and the federal government rather than state governors, and they can be commanded by regular army officers. This is sometimes called "Title 10 status" because it is explained and mandated under Title 10 of the US Code, which defines both the general

WEEKEND WARRIORS

Members of the National Guard are sometimes referred to as "weekend warriors." This nickname comes from the fact that members of the guard train only one weekend a month and two weeks a year. The term is less accurate now that so many guard troops have been called to active duty for months at a time.

THE ORGANIZATION OF THE US NATIONAL GUARD

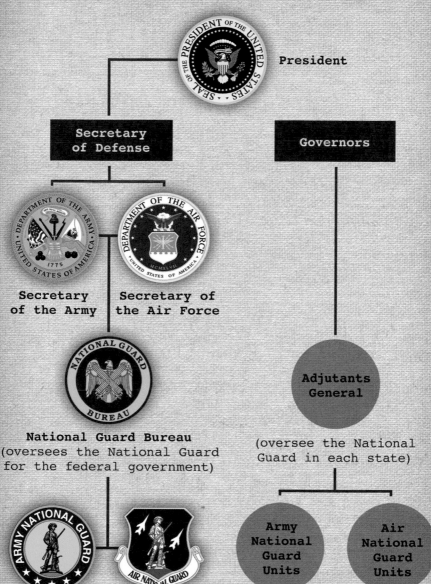

President

Secretary of Defense

Governors

Secretary of the Army

Secretary of the Air Force

National Guard Bureau
(oversees the National Guard for the federal government)

Army National Guard

Air National Guard

Adjutants General

(oversee the National Guard in each state)

Army National Guard Units

Air National Guard Units

Minnesota Army National Guard members assisted with crowd control during the 2008 Republican National Convention in Saint Paul, Minnesota.

and permanent laws of the United States. Guard members can be federalized because of a national emergency declared by the president, when the president feels it is necessary to augment regular military troops or to use guard troops to enforce federal laws. The president can also activate National Guard units if a state rebels against the government or when citizens interfere with state or federal laws.

TWENTY-FIRST CENTURY MISSIONS

Following the events of September 11, 2001, the National Guard began operating under Title 10 status more frequently than it had since the end of the Vietnam War.

In 2002, President George W. Bush's administration released a report called *The National Strategy for Homeland Security*. This strategy had three objectives: to prevent terrorist attacks within the United States, to reduce the country's vulnerability to terrorist attacks, and to minimize the damage done by any attacks and help the country recover from them quickly.

How did this affect the National Guard? There were two viewpoints. One was that the guard should be strengthened and take on homeland security and defense as its primary mission. Others thought the guard should be mobilized as reserve troops to support the regular military in conflicts overseas. In the end, both of these things happened. To defend against future terrorist air attacks, a new homeland security mission called Operation Noble Eagle rejuvenated the country's minimal air defense

HOMELAND DEFENSE

The National Guard performed a vital role ensuring homeland security after the terrorist attacks of September 11, 2001. Immediately after the attacks, 9,000 guard members increased security at 422 commercial airports.[2] Guard members also inspected more than 100 suspicious letters and packages that might have contained explosives or chemical agents. Guard troops added security at all border crossings with Mexico and Canada. In Washington, DC, they provided added security for government buildings, especially the US Capitol and the White House. Guard members have also served on security details at the World Series, the New York City Marathon, and the Olympic Games to make sure people are secure while attending these popular events. And when terrorists bombed the Boston Marathon in 2013, guard members immediately swung into action, helping the injured and assisting with evacuation.

CURRENT MISSION

The National Guard's mission today is more important than ever before in US history. According to Mary Corbett, author of *National Guard 101*, the guard exists for these reasons:

- *To provide security and defense to the US homeland both here and abroad*
- *To support the Global War on Terrorism, both at home and abroad*
- *To provide the United States with a relevant, reliable, and ready force that has been transformed to meet the needs of the 21st century*[3]

system. The ANG patrols US air space and remains on alert for any aerial security threats. The National Guard has also activated its troops for active combat duties in Iraq and Afghanistan.

In 2001, the United States and other allied nations launched attacks on Afghanistan with the code name Operation Enduring Freedom. The guard and regular US military personnel have continued serving in Afghanistan, although President Barack Obama announced in 2011 the United States planned to withdraw all troops by the end of 2014. Guard troops continue serving in Iraq as well. Leaders of the regular army command have said the United States would not be able to maintain its presence in Iraq without National Guard troops.

Guard members now routinely serve an average of 18 months on overseas duty. This has changed the public's image of guard members as casual soldiers who perform their one weekend a month and two weeks a

An A-10 Thunderbolt II from the Arkansas Air National Guard's 188th Fighter Wing performs a midair refueling mission over Egypt on October 12, 2012.

year minimal guard duty. Today the public sees guard members as trained soldiers who have been involved in the wars and missions in the Middle East since 2002. According to William Boehm, National Guard historian, "One of the [changes] has been the transformation of the National Guard into, in a larger sense, a much more ready fighting force, instead of a strategic reserve, which it has historically been throughout the twentieth century."[4]

CHAPTER SIX
SERVICE AT HOME

hile military missions in Iraq and Afghanistan have made the public increasingly aware of the National Guard's role in conflicts overseas, many Americans are more familiar with their role during times of disaster and unrest here at home.

A National Guard convoy arrived in Coney Island, New York, to help residents after Hurricane Sandy.

Often when a major disaster strikes anywhere in the United States, National Guard troops are called out to assist in search and rescue, security, medical, and peacekeeping roles. While serving in a disaster may be different from fighting a war on foreign soil, dealing with these missions requires the same high level of training and performance. A disaster, whether natural or man-made, is any event that overwhelms the ability of local and state authorities to respond to it. Disasters can include natural events such as hurricanes, earthquakes, fires, and floods. Man-made disasters include events such as large-scale outages of electric power, chemical spills, or radiation accidents.

Every state in the country has established disaster plans and some sort of an office to provide emergency services. When a disaster occurs, that office or agency is responsible for coordinating emergency relief and disaster response efforts, reporting directly to the governor of

The Michigan National Guard used an aerial firefighting tool suspended below a helicopter to extinguish a wildfire ten miles (16 km) from Tahquamenon Falls State Park on August 8, 2007.

NATIONAL GUARD
STATE PARTNERSHIPS

National Guard
partner countries

The National Guard State Partnership Program (SPP)
is a US Department of Defense program managed
by the National Guard that links US states with
partner countries around the world.

the state. Local emergency services such as police and firefighters are the first to respond in a disaster, followed by state organizations and then the state's National Guard.

When a disaster occurs, the state mobilizes its emergency operations office. Sometimes this can happen even before a disaster takes place. This is the case with hurricanes, which can be predicted and tracked more easily than other disasters such as tornados or earthquakes. The emergency office gathers information, assesses the damage, and then advises the governor about what needs to be done.

If the situation is bad enough, the governor will then ask the president to declare a disaster. If the president does so, the federal government pays the costs of the guard's deployment and active duty during these times. Once an official federal disaster is declared, other states' guard units can also be activated. Some disasters require the mobilization of National Guard troops only within the state that is directly affected. Other disasters, such as Hurricanes Rita and Katrina in 2005, or the terrorist

KATRINA BY THE NUMBERS

The National Guard played a huge role during Hurricane Katrina, and a quick look at the numbers proves it. According to Lou Dolinar, in his article "Katrina: What the Media Missed," the guard's presence in New Orleans included:

- "At least 2,500 troops who rode out the storm inside the city
- A dozen emergency shelters
- More than 200 boats and dozens of high-water vehicles
- 10,244 sorties flown
- 88,181 passengers moved
- 18,834 tons of cargo hauled"[1]

attacks of September 11, 2001, require the activation of guard soldiers from many different states.

The National Guard is also sometimes called on to work with the Federal Emergency Management Agency (FEMA). FEMA has the authority to call up both National Guard and reserve troops, as well as regular military, in times of disaster.

DART

In 2009, the National Guard created two special disaster response teams to cope with truly catastrophic disasters that would overwhelm local authorities and require a federal response. These disasters include events such as major disease outbreaks and powerful hurricanes. These teams would also respond in the event of man-made disasters such as the detonation of a nuclear bomb, the release of a disease agent such as anthrax, or chemical or explosive attacks.

These special response teams include guard members with specific knowledge or training regarding how to respond to 15 different possible disaster scenarios. These guard members often have disaster-related skills learned in their civilian jobs as well. Called District All-Hazard Response Teams (DART) East and West, these two teams each cover half of the United States. The teams have special "packages" of troops and equipment

"I AM THE GUARD"

The National Guard's motto describes the many vital roles the citizen soldiers of the United States fill:

I Am the Guard: Civilian in Peace, Soldier in War . . . of security and honor for three centuries I have been the custodian . . . I am the Guard!

Civilian in peace, soldier in war . . . the stricken have known the comfort of my skill. I have faced forward to the tornado, the typhoon, and the horror of the hurricane and the flood. I saw the tall towers fall—I was there!

I am the Guard. For three centuries the custodian of security and honor, now and forever . . . I am the Guard.[2]

assets across the country they can easily access. These resources include army and ANG members, special response teams, aviation equipment, military police, engineers, medical personnel and supplies, and communications equipment. DART teams practice by creating disaster scenarios and running drills so they can learn how to cope with these dangerous situations. They practice for both unexpected scenarios and more common situations so they will be prepared for anything that might happen.

UNITY OF ACTION

The need to establish more effective chains of command and communication during disasters was made plain after Hurricane Katrina in 2005. Fifty thousand National Guard members from all over the country, as well as regular civilian emergency response professionals and military members, came to assist New Orleans and the surrounding area damaged by the hurricane. It quickly became apparent to everyone involved that it would be difficult to coordinate all these different groups, each of which had its own commanders or authorities.

In 2011, the Department of Defense created a special plan for dealing with disasters called Unity of Action. When a disaster takes place, that state's governor usually supervises all response efforts, including the National Guard. But under the Unity of Action plan, a guard officer is called in to work with the governor as a dual-status commander. This means he or she commands not only the responding guard units but also any regular military units that respond to the emergency. This commander also works closely with the state governor. In fact, such

New Jersey National Guard member Andrea Pittman offloads diesel fuel from a heavy expanded mobility tactical truck (HEMTT) in November 2012 as part of the response to Hurricane Sandy.

a commander is ideally selected and trained before any disaster occurs, giving this individual time to establish a relationship with the state's governor so they can work together more effectively if a disaster strikes. Said Nebraska governor Dave Heineman, this policy has "helped further establish trust between the governors and the Department of Defense and it is providing the foundation for a new, stronger partnership between state and federal military forces. [It is] the cornerstone for a successful emergency response effort."[3]

KEEPING THE PEACE

Guard units continually train for situations in which they might be called on to supply help or restore order. Some units have performed drills in which they prepare to deal with an epidemic. These citizen soldiers train to care for and control sick people and provide medicine and other supplies. Other guard members train for scenarios in which widespread power outages lead to various emergencies. These soldiers learn how to deliver food and drinking water to people who no longer have access to such necessities.

Disasters at home, both natural and man-made, sometimes require the National Guard to deal with criminal activities such as looting and theft that occur when regular law enforcement agencies are not operating and circumstances have made people more likely to commit crimes. The guard is also sometimes called out in response to large-scale protests or riots.

In 1992, the guard responded when some neighborhoods in Los Angeles, California, erupted in riots. This unrest was sparked when the policemen charged with beating an African-American motorist named Rodney King were acquitted of that crime. At least 53 people died and there was an estimated $1 billion of property damage before the California National Guard restored order.[4]

The National Guard plays many vital roles in the United States. From defending its people against terrorism or foreign enemies both at home and overseas to providing disaster relief and restoring order, these volunteers are true citizen soldiers.

ON THE BORDER

In May 2006, President George W. Bush authorized a new mission for the guard. National Guard members reinforced the US Customs and Border Patrol in an effort to create more secure borders between the United States and neighboring countries. This was done partly in an effort to prevent undocumented immigrants from entering the country. Guard members now perform aerial reconnaissance missions along these borders and help construct and maintain fences, roads, lights, towers, and sensing equipment.

CHAPTER SEVEN

WEAPONS AND EQUIPMENT

The men and women of the National Guard play many roles, from soldier to peacekeeper to emergency service provider. These different roles require a variety of gear, technology, and weapons. The National Guard and the ANG use the same equipment and vehicles as regular military forces.

National Guardsmen train for combat during an air assault exercise at Fort Drum, New York, on August 13, 2013.

The US Code mandates that military personnel must wear the proper uniforms specified for their branch of the service. Service (or dress) uniforms for guard members consist of white shirts, dark blue pants for men and skirts for women, and a dark blue uniform jacket. Combat uniforms consist of a jacket, pants, patrol cap, T-shirt,

THE ORIGIN OF CAMOUFLAGE PATTERNS

Camouflage uniforms were first developed during World War I, when trench and aerial warfare made it necessary to conceal soldiers from the enemy. The army designers who first created camouflage patterns relied on a book by naturalist Abbott Thayer called *Concealing Coloration in the Animal Kingdom*. Artists Grant Wood and Jacques Villon also helped develop cloth patterns that would fool the eye. The word *camouflage* is borrowed from the French word *camoufler*, meaning "to disguise."

and combat boots. A hard-shell helmet replaces the patrol cap in combat situations.

Except for the T-shirt, which is either sand colored or green, and the tan boots, a guard member's combat uniform is made of camouflage-patterned fabric. The current camouflage, called Universal Camouflage Pattern (UCP), is a tan, gray, and green pattern with a pixelated look. This pattern is intended to blend in with any kind of environment, including deserts, woodlands, and urban areas. Some soldiers in Afghanistan are now wearing a different camouflage pattern called Multicam, which has an irregular greenish-brown look. These new patterns are designed to work well in desert environments.

Guard members sometimes wear bulletproof vests in combat situations. These are vests that use ceramic plates or layers of woven fabrics such as Kevlar to protect the wearer from bullets and shrapnel. Guard members also need protective gear to wear in the event of chemical or nuclear attacks. These include special protective masks and sensing systems that can identify dangerous chemical and biological agents or radiation in the air. Guard members also have special suits that protect them from chemical weapons, radioactive fallout, or other battlefield contamination.

INSIGNIA AND RANK

A soldier's rank and group are indicated by insignia on his or her uniforms. Each rank has its own insignia. This indicates what that soldier's rank is and where he or she falls in the command structure. Guard members also wear patches that indicate the division or state unit to which they belong, as well as any major campaigns in which they have participated, such as duty in Iraq or Afghanistan.

Ranks in the National Guard and the ANG are the same as in the regular army and air force. According to the Department of Defense, rank is extremely important: "Military rank is more than just who salutes whom.

Military rank is a badge of leadership. Responsibility for personnel, equipment, and mission grows with each increase in rank."[1]

WEAPONS

As with the regular army, the National Guard has many types of weapons in its arsenals, from small arms to bombs, missiles, and artillery. Individual weapons include a bayonet that can be used as a knife or attached to an M-14 rifle. Soldiers can also carry an M-9 pistol, an M-4 carbine, or an M-16 rifle, which is air-cooled and gas-operated and can be used as either a semiautomatic or fully automatic weapon. Other weapons include the M19-3 grenade rifle, the M203 grenade launcher, the M240B machine gun, and the M249 squad automatic weapon (SAW), which allows a single person to deliver a large number of bullets.

The Javelin and TOW (tube-launched, optically tracked, wire command–link guided) missile systems are weapons that can be used against armored vehicles such as tanks. These weapons can be operated by one soldier, although the TOW is often mounted on vehicles as well. The guard also uses larger artillery weapons such as howitzers and mortars that can send rockets and missiles over longer distances. These weapons are called indirect fire systems because the soldier operating them is not close to his or her target. There are also several types of air defense artillery, such as the Patriot and the Avenger, which can launch missiles at attacking aircraft.

GETTING AROUND

Both the army and National Guard units have special vehicles that can be used either for attack or as protection from attack. These include several types of tanks, armored vehicles, and personnel carriers that operate on tracks instead of wheels, making them effective in rugged or uneven terrain.

The guard also uses wheeled vehicles including tactical vehicles, trucks, and the high-mobility multipurpose wheeled vehicle (HMMWV), otherwise known as the Humvee. This large vehicle can carry men or missiles and serves as a scout vehicle or ambulance. Another guard

A member of the Georgia National Guard disassembles an M249 SAW as part of a Best Warrior Competition.

A Virginia National Guard UH-72 helicopter aircrew conducts training with a local fire and rescue team at the Chesterfield County Public Safety Training Center in Chester, Virginia, on May 15, 2013.

vehicle, called the Palletized Load System, is a truck with a trailer that can automatically load and unload cargo such as containers and other heavy loads. The Stryker, which comes in several versions, is an armored vehicle designed to move quickly in urban terrain that can still protect its occupants in open areas.

The National Guard also uses several types of helicopters, including the Apache, Chinook, Blackhawk, and Kiowa Warrior. The ANG has access to the same airplanes as the air force, including fighter planes, jets, bombers, and cargo planes, as well as a wide variety of self-propelled missiles.

HIGH-TECH WARRIORS

The National Guard and the army have many weapons and types of equipment that make use of the newest technology. Guard members can use infrared and laser targeting systems to find targets and guide bombs to specific locations. Unmanned armored vehicles, spy planes, and even robots can be used in situations in which a human soldier might be put in danger. Special body armor made from ceramic materials offers more protection from enemy fire.

Because of the increasingly technical knowledge needed to operate some of the weapons, vehicles, and equipment used by the National Guard, it is even more important than ever for guard troops to receive comprehensive training in their particular job. This means there are a wide variety of jobs and even long-term careers available to those men and women who choose to join the ranks of the National Guard.

CITY IN A BOX

One of the newer technologies that benefits guard troops in the field is called the City in a Box. This is a prefabricated, modular, self-sustaining city that can house up to 550 troops and covers seven to ten acres (3 to 4 ha) of land. This equipment can be tailored to the specific needs of individual units and missions. The basic unit of these cities is called the "Tent Extendable Modular Personnel" (TEMPER) tent. This soldier housing even has heating and air conditioning. Sixty people can set up one of these temporary cities in a week, and they have been used in deployments all over the world.

CHAPTER EIGHT
CAREER OPPORTUNITIES

Being a member of the National Guard is not a one-size-fits-all arrangement. Because the guard, like the regular army, requires its members to perform a wide variety of tasks, guard members must find their own particular role based on what they want to do and the tasks to which they are best suited. While one guard

Tennessee National Guard troops participate in training in preparation for a scheduled deployment to Iraq.

member may excel in communications technology, for example, another might be very good at marksmanship. Each of these individuals can find a job with the guard that will fit his or her strengths and abilities. After basic training, guard members can choose from more than 150 jobs in a variety of career fields.

ABILITY TEST

Many high school students who are interested in enlisting in the military have the chance to take the ASVAB test while they are still in school. The ASVAB isn't a test a student can pass or fail. It is instead a measurement of ability. Students do have to achieve a minimum score (which varies depending on the branch of the military in which they're interested). Students' ASVAB scores reflect their abilities and knowledge compared with other men and women in their age group. ASVAB scores are good for only two years. After that, if a student has not joined the military, he or she will have to take the test again before enlisting in the National Guard.

Because jobs in the National Guard often correspond to similar jobs in the civilian world, serving as a guard member can also be a good way to gain real-world job skills and prepare for a civilian career. In fact, almost every job in the civilian world has a similar counterpart in the National Guard. However, many guard members continue working in a regular civilian career while also serving as a part of the guard, using their skills in support of national security and disaster response when needed.

THE ASVAB

Before enlisting, potential guard recruits must take a test called the Armed Services Vocational Aptitude Battery (ASVAB). This exam can be taken either on a computer or as a standard paper-and-pencil test. The ASVAB measures general science knowledge, mathematical reasoning and knowledge, vocabulary, reading comprehension, knowledge of automobiles and vehicle repair, mechanical comprehension, and electronics knowledge. The computer version of the test also has a section that tests the recruit's ability to assemble parts of an object.

The score a potential citizen soldier receives on the ASVAB will determine the jobs that particular recruit might be eligible for in the guard. It is not just an intelligence test but also a test of skills and comprehension.

A WIDE RANGE OF PATHS

Once a recruit has taken the ASVAB and there is some indication of the tasks for which he or she might be suited, it's time to look at the jobs available. In the National Guard, these jobs fall into three categories: combat

UNEMPLOYMENT AND THE GUARD

Some guard members find it hard to find jobs once they are done with active duty. Sometimes they have difficulty translating the things they have learned in the military into skills employers find useful. Some employers are leery of hiring guard members because they might be redeployed in the future. Many guard members who find themselves in this kind of situation reenlist for further tours of active duty in places like Iraq or Afghanistan simply as a way to find employment and support their families. While some guard members struggle to translate their military skills into regular jobs, these individuals often have a lot to offer. Ross Cohen is the director of the Hiring Our Heroes program, which holds job fairs to help guard veterans find new jobs in the civilian world. Cohen was quoted in an article in *USA Today* as saying,

> Employers need to know that you also learn to work well in teams, give and take orders, be accountable for millions of dollars of equipment, and respond to changing circumstances.[1]

arms (CA), combat support (CS), and combat service support (CSS). Each category fulfills a specific military function. Some guard jobs fall under more than one of these categories.

CA jobs include armor positions, which enable the guard to strike quickly in military battle operations with tanks, cavalry, or reconnaissance operations. Those recruits who go into field artillery, also a CA job, must learn to use strategic weapons such as long-range cannons, rockets, and missiles to neutralize or suppress the enemy. Infantry jobs, the first line of defense in military operations, are also CA jobs, as is aviation.

CS jobs include working as an engineer in construction and demolition projects, the mechanical jobs that are part of aviation, and signal jobs, a category that includes any job relating to communication and information systems. Military intelligence, a function in which guard members gather, report, and analyze information about political situations and other countries, is also a CS job, as is service with the military police.

CSS jobs include other types of aviation and engineering positions, certain signaling and military police jobs, transporting soldiers around the country or around the world, medical jobs, logistics support, machinery and equipment maintenance, working as an interpreter or translator, and performing administrative work such

A Hawaii National Guardsman tests one of four CH-47 Chinook helicopters for use in support of an army mission in Africa.

as managing records, payroll, and news reporting. These types of jobs may not take place on the front lines in times of armed conflict, but they make it possible for combat troops to perform efficiently.

There are also careers in the National Guard that require members to already have advanced training in a career field—usually one they perform in the civilian world—or receive more intensive training within the

A chaplain from the Georgia National Guard worked with schoolchildren from the Ududui Primary School near Soroti, Uganda, during an outreach visit.

guard. These include medical careers, legal jobs, and jobs for chaplains, who provide religious support to the troops.

THE IMPORTANCE OF RANK

Rank is a way of organizing military members by experience, occupation, and education. Most important, it establishes the chain of command, so everyone knows who is in charge at each level. Since the National Guard's organizational structure is the same as that of the regular army, guard units are able to merge seamlessly with army units during times of armed conflict. Their roles and responsibilities are already established, and they can get to work immediately without having to determine how they fit in with established army soldiers and jobs.

The lowest rank in the National Guard, as well as in the regular army, is a private. The highest rank is that of

ARMY NATIONAL GUARD RANKS

Enlisted

Private
Private 2
Private First Class
Specialist
Corporal
Sergeant
Staff Sergeant
Sergeant First Class
Master Sergeant
First Sergeant
Sergeant Major
Command Sergeant Major
Sergeant Major of the Army

Warrant Officer

Warrant Officer
Chief Warrant Officer 2
Chief Warrant Officer 3
Chief Warrant Officer 4
Chief Warrant Officer 5

Officer

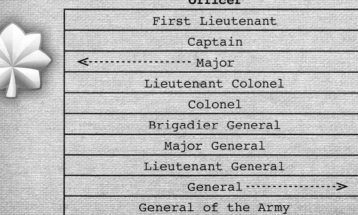

First Lieutenant
Captain
Major
Lieutenant Colonel
Colonel
Brigadier General
Major General
Lieutenant General
General
General of the Army

general or, in times of war, the general of the army. Rank also determines how much guard members are paid, as well as determining the personnel and equipment for which they are responsible.

Guard members can gain rank through experience, as well as further training and education. The National Guard has an active promotion system. It is possible to join the guard right out of high school as a private and then work one's way up through the ranking system to become a noncommissioned or even regular officer.

The jobs one can undertake in the National Guard, as well as the pay and rank associated with them, sometimes depend on whether a recruit is an enlisted soldier or an officer. Officers generally enter the service having already received a college education. However, a recruit with only a high school diploma can receive additional training through leadership schools within the guard to become a noncommissioned officer. Leadership schools include the Warrior Leader Course, Advanced Leader Course, Senior

NONCOMMISSIONED v. COMMISSIONED

What is the difference between a noncommissioned officer and a commissioned officer in the army and National Guard? A noncommissioned officer is a soldier who works his or her way up through the ranks through training and experience over time. A commissioned officer is someone who has a college degree, may have completed Reserve Officers' Training Corps (ROTC) training during college, attended Officer Candidate School or a US military academy, or already has a professional credential in law, medicine, or religion when he or she joins the military.

Leader Course, First Sergeant Course, and Sergeants Major Course. By taking these courses, a recruit can gain rank and become an officer without having to first earn college credits.

There are three categories of officers within the National Guard: branch officers, specialty officers, and warrant officers. Branch officers serve in the CA branch (infantry, armor, and field artillery), the CS branch (military police, signal, and military intelligence), or the CSS branch (finance, transportation, and quartermasters). Specialty officers have specialized, professional skills. These guard members include medical professionals, chaplains, and judge advocate general (JAG) officers. Warrant officers are subject-matter experts in specific technical areas. They are not commissioned officers and do not need a college degree, but they must have five to seven years of experience in the guard.

JAG

JAG is short for judge advocate general. These are officers who already have law degrees and have passed the bar exam in their state. This means they are already professional lawyers. They then receive additional training within the National Guard or army in the specific requirements of army and military law. Some JAG officers enlist to receive additional experience and training. Others remain in the military for their entire careers.

CHAPTER NINE
LIFE IN THE NATIONAL GUARD

The day-to-day life of a member of the National Guard depends on many factors, including what the soldier's job is and whether he or she is deployed in the United States or overseas. Soldiers' lives will also change depending on whether they are performing routine

National Guardsmen from South Carolina combined forces with members of the Japan Ground Self-Defense Force during joint training in Japan.

missions, undergoing training, responding to a natural disaster, or participating in a military action in a war zone. It is the type of mission in which a soldier is engaged that determines what his or her daily life is like.

A member of the Puerto Rico Army National Guard undergoes weapons qualification testing.

BECOMING A PART OF THE GUARD

Everyone who joins the National Guard must first go through basic combat training. Here recruits go through a medical exam and orientations. They then learn combat skills and receive fitness training. Every guard member, regardless of what position he or she later holds, must be a soldier first, ready and able to fight.

After basic training, National Guard members are given assignments based on their aptitudes, their scores on the ASVAB, and the needs of the guard at the time. But since the citizen soldiers of the guard are not full-time members of the US military, many of them still hold full-time jobs or attend school even after joining the guard. They attend training and drills one weekend out of every month and two weeks a year. But when there is a disaster or security issue, guard members can be called to duty.

REWARDS

Air Force Command Chief Master Sergeant Vincent Morton, the senior enlisted leader of the New Jersey Air National Guard, talked about what it felt like to help Hurricane Sandy victims in his own state in 2012:

We bring a calming effect. Outside the door, the wind is blowing, the tide is coming up, when they see us in uniform, it brings that calming effect. We get an opportunity to serve right here in the State of New Jersey. It's our neighbors. It's very rewarding. You go overseas, you serve your country—but it's even more rewarding when you get back and you serve your neighbors. The Air National Guard is a key piece when there's a state emergency, we're always easy to get to, and we bring a huge skill set to the fight.[1]

ACTIVATION

National Guard units are usually put on alert months before they are actually called up for service. This gives members time to prepare their families and to communicate with their employers, schools, landlords, and other people who need to know they may be gone for some time. If a guard member is going to be put on active duty for more than 30 days, he or she must be given at least 30 days' notice beforehand. The secretary of defense can waive this rule, however, in times of national emergency as declared by the president or Congress. And in some cases (such as a natural disaster), a guard unit may be activated only hours or days after being put on alert.

All National Guard units have a telephone alert notification system that tells members they are being called up for service. These phone calls are followed by

Illinois National Guard recruits stand for inspection.

A DAY IN THE LIFE: BASIC COMBAT TRAINING

What is it like for a new National Guard member to attend basic combat training? Training takes place at the nearest army or guard facility. New recruits spend the first four to five days in an area known as reception battalion. Here new guard members fill out paperwork, undergo medical exams, and receive their ID cards, uniforms, and other gear. They also receive vaccinations and glasses, if needed.

Next comes basic combat training, where new guard members learn the skills they need to become soldiers. Basic training takes ten weeks and starts with what is known as Shakedown, during which soldiers learn to follow instructions. Next comes classroom training, in which soldiers learn the history of the army and its core values. Then recruits move on to what is called the White Phase, where they learn basic marksmanship, rappelling, hand-to-hand combat, night operation protocols, compass reading, and other skills. In what is called the Blue Phase, soldiers train in more specific subject areas, such as fighting in urban terrain, handling explosives, marching over long distances, and more advanced types of weapons.

At the end of training, soldiers must pass an End of Cycle exam that includes 212 tasks and an army physical fitness test.

a certified letter or other type of message informing the guard member that he or she is going to be called to active duty. If an employer or school has questions about activation, they can contact the guard member's commanding officer.

ANG and National Guard units are usually activated as a group, with the entire unit being called to service at one time. But sometimes guard members are activated as individuals. This usually happens if a particular guard member is attending special training, is a subject-matter expert needed on a particular mission, or is performing duties such as notifying family members of a soldier's death.

According to the Uniformed Services Employment and Reemployment Rights Act, guard members who also have regular employment cannot be discriminated against by their employers. This means guard members have the right to return to their jobs when they are no longer on active duty as long as they let their employer know in advance and are not dishonorably discharged from military service.

EMPLOYERS GET A TASTE

Because a good relationship between a guard member and his regular employer is so important, some guard units hold special events to give employers a taste of what it's like to serve in the guard. These events may include mock operations and combat, riding in helicopters, and engaging in simulated firefights. These events give employers a better sense of what guard members do, as well as an understanding of how vital these individuals are to national defense.

Employers are also required to excuse guard members to attend training and drills. However, an employer only has to support an employee's military service for a total of five years of active duty away from their regular jobs.

RISKS AND BENEFITS

Serving as a member of the National Guard has both risks and benefits. Members can use their guard time to learn skills that will help them build a career in the civilian world. They can earn money to use for college. They may also have the opportunity to travel both in the United States and overseas. And they of course have the satisfaction of helping their country and fellow Americans during times of war and in cases of natural disaster or civil unrest.

However, being a member of the guard also means being a member of the military. Guard members cannot refuse overseas duty simply because they do not want to find themselves in a combat zone. They may be deployed to battle zones such as Afghanistan or Iraq, and they may be injured or killed. Being a guard member can also be hard on families and relationships, since soldiers may have to be away from home for long periods of time, sometimes without very much warning, and may return home in need of extensive medical or mental health care.

A member of the Virginia National Guard reunites with loved ones after serving on federal active duty in Afghanistan for almost a year.

Being a member of the National Guard is ultimately a way to be a vital part of the US military in both war and peace without joining the regular military. For many guard members, knowing they can have a normal civilian life while also having the opportunity to serve their country makes service in the guard one of the most rewarding things they do. And at a time in history when there are many new threats, defending the United States is more important than ever.

HELPING GUARD FAMILIES

The National Guard has an established program to help the families of their members cope with the responsibilities of their loved one's service. The National Guard Family Program helps guard members and their families deal with issues such as overseas deployment and health care. This program also prepares families for what it will be like when a loved one is called up, supports and educates guard families, and works for the well-being of all guard family members, from children to adults. There is a National Guard Family Program in every state in the country.

TIMELINE

1607

The first citizen soldier militias of the American colonies are created at the Jamestown settlement in Virginia.

1620

The Pilgrims establish a militia at Plymouth.

1636

On December 13, the first official militia regiment is founded in Massachusetts. This date eventually becomes the official birthday of the National Guard.

1775

On April 19, the Colonial militia defeats the British at Lexington and Concord, Massachusetts, starting the Revolutionary War.

1861–1865

The Confederate States and the Union fight the Civil War. Militia groups played a significant role for both the Southern and Northern war efforts.

1903

The Militia Act of 1903 converts the volunteer militia into the National Guard.

1917
The National Guard is activated to fight in World War I.

1941–1945
The United States fights in World War II. Several National Guard units play a significant combat role during the war.

1990–1991
National Guard units serve during the Persian Gulf War and Operation Desert Storm.

2001
The National Guard is activated on September 11 after the terrorist attacks on the United States.

2005
The National Guard is called out to assist victims of Hurricane Katrina.

2012
The National Guard assists victims of Hurricane Sandy.

ESSENTIAL FACTS

DATE OF FOUNDING
December 13, 1636

MOTTO
"Always ready, always there"

PERSONNEL (2013)
More than 460,000

ROLE
The National Guard performs missions for national defense and security, including responding to civil unrest and natural disasters, military threats to the United States, and terrorist attacks against US interests.

SIGNIFICANT MISSIONS
American Revolution, 1775–1783
American Civil War, 1861–1865
World War I, 1917–1918
Response to Japanese attack on Pearl Harbor, 1941
Operation Desert Storm, 1991
Response to Hurricanes Katrina and Sandy, 2005 and 2012

WELL-KNOWN NATIONAL GUARDSMEN

Captain Miles Standish of Plymouth, Massachusetts, established the first militia.

Future president George Washington served in a colonial militia.

Paul Revere alerted the militias to meet British forces at the start of the Revolutionary War.

Captain Isaac Davis served and died during the Revolutionary War, and his likeness has become a symbol of the National Guard.

Senator Charles W. F. Dick improved funding for the National Guard at the start of the 1900s.

The nurses of the "Kirkuk Seven" helped capture former Iraqi president Saddam Hussein in 2003.

QUOTE

"Every Man therefore that wishes to secure his own Freedom, and thinks it his Duty to defend that of his Country, should, as he prides himself in being a Free Citizen, think it his truest Honour to be a Soldier Citizen." —*Exercise for the Militia of the Province of Massachusetts Bay*, Boston, 1758

GLOSSARY

ACTIVATE
To make a military unit or group operational or send it on a mission.

AUGMENT
To make something greater by adding to it.

CIVILIAN
A person who is not a member of the military.

DEPLOY
To move troops into position for military action.

ENLIST
To enroll in or join the armed services or military.

GARRISON
Manning a permanent military base.

INSURRECTION
A violent uprising against an authority or government.

INTELLIGENCE
A collection of information that has military or political value.

MANDATORY
Required by laws or rules.

MILITIA
A group of citizens organized for military service.

MOBILIZATION
The assembly of troops and their preparation for war or an emergency.

PARAMEDIC
A person who is trained to do medical work but is not a doctor.

RECONNAISSANCE
Scouting or surveying, especially in wartime.

RELEGATE
To send or dismiss to an inferior rank or position.

STANDING ARMY
A permanent army of paid soldiers.

THEATER
An area of land, sea, or air that is involved in a war.

ADDITIONAL RESOURCES

SELECTED BIBLIOGRAPHY

Corbett, Mary. *National Guard 101: A Handbook for Spouses*. New York: Savas Beatie, 2011. Print.

Doubler, Michael D. *The National Guard and Reserve: A Reference Handbook*. Westport, CT: Praeger Security International, 2008. Print.

Doubler, Michael D., and John W. Listman Jr. *The National Guard: An Illustrated History of America's Citizen-Soldiers*. 2nd ed. Washington, DC: Potomac, 2007. Print.

FURTHER READINGS

Grayson, Robert. *Revolutionary War*. Minneapolis: ABDO, 2014. Print.

Nathan, Amy. *Count on Us: American Women in the Military*. Washington, DC: National Geographic Children's, 2004. Print.

Reef, Catherine. *African Americans in the Military*. New York: Infobase, 2010. Print.

WEBSITES

To learn more about Essential Library of the US Military, visit **booklinks.abdopublishing.com**. These links are routinely monitored and updated to provide the most current information available.

PLACES TO VISIT

MINUTE MAN NATIONAL HISTORICAL PARK

174 Liberty Street

Concord, MA 01742

978-369-6993

http://www.nps.gov/mima/index.htm

Located outside of Boston, Massachusetts, in the towns of Lincoln, Lexington, and Concord, this park includes the sites of the first battles of the American Revolution, a theater and information center, and a trail that follows the path taken by the minutemen in April 1775.

THE NATIONAL GUARD MEMORIAL MUSEUM

One Massachusetts Avenue, NW

Washington, DC 20001

202-789-0031

http://www.ngaus.org/national-guard-memorial-museum#sthash.Gj0GVv9Z.dpuf

This is the only museum dedicated to the history of the US citizen soldier and the National Guard. In addition to exhibits and artifacts, the museum is also involved in community outreach efforts and runs educational programs.

SOURCE NOTES

CHAPTER 1. AT GROUND ZERO

1. Major Les Melnyk. "Interviews: Ranauro." *The New York National Guard and 9-11.* New York State Division of Military and Naval Affairs, n.d. Web. 30 Mar. 2014.
2. Ibid.
3. Ibid.
4. Lisa Daniel. "Recruiters Recall Patriotism of Post-9/11 America." *US Department of Defense.* US Department of Defense, 8 Sept. 2011. Web. 30 Mar. 2014.
5. "Saffir-Simpson Hurricane Scale." *National Oceanographic & Meteorological Laboratory.* National Oceanographic & Meteorological Laboratory, n.d. Web. 30 Mar. 2014.
6. Tech. Sgt. John Orrell, USAF. "Hurricane Katrina Response: National Guard's 'Finest Hour.'" *US Army.* US Army, 27 Aug. 2010. Web. 30 Mar. 2014.
7. "Soldier's Creed." *US Army.* US Army, n.d. Web. 30 Mar. 2014.
8. Tech. Sgt. John Orrell, USAF. "Hurricane Katrina Response: National Guard's 'Finest Hour.'" *US Army.* US Army, 27 Aug. 2010. Web. 30 Mar. 2014.
9. Ibid.
10. Ibid.
11. "ARNG by the Numbers." *Army National Guard.* Army National Guard, 6 Mar. 2014. Web. 1 Apr. 2014.
12. "Our Services." *US Department of Defense.* US Department of Defense, n.d. Web. 1 Apr. 2014.

CHAPTER 2. MINUTEMEN TO MILITIA

1. Michael D. Doubler. *Civilian in Peace, Soldier in War.* Lawrence, KS: UP of Kansas, 2003. Print. 17.
2. Ibid. 31–35.
3. Ibid. 3.
4. Ibid. 31.
5. Ibid. 35.
6. "The Battle of Bunker Hill 1775." *BritishBattles.com.* BritishBattles.com, n.d. Web. 30 Mar. 2014.
7. "The Real Story of Revere's Ride." *The Paul Revere House.* Paul Revere Memorial Association, n.d. Web. 30 Mar. 2014.
8. Michael D. Doubler. *The National Guard: An Illustrated History of America's Citizen-Soldiers.* Dulles, VA: Potomac, 2007. Print. 19.
9. Bob Johnson. "Remember Minuteman Isaac Davis." *Veteran's Today Military & Foreign Affairs Journal.* Veteran's Today, 19 Apr. 2012. Web. 30 Mar. 2014.
10. Ibid.

11. Michael D. Doubler. *Civilian in Peace, Soldier in War*. Lawrence, KS: UP of Kansas, 2003. Print. 97.

12. Michael D. Doubler. *The National Guard: An Illustrated History of America's Citizen-Soldiers*. Dulles, VA: Potomac, 2007. Print. 19.

13. Michael D. Doubler. *Civilian in Peace, Soldier in War*. Lawrence, KS: UP of Kansas, 2003. Print. 121.

CHAPTER 3. WORLD WARS AND BEYOND

1. Michael D. Doubler. *Civilian in Peace, Soldier in War*. Lawrence, KS: UP of Kansas, 2003. Print. 144–146.

2. Ibid. 159–160.

3. Ibid.

4. Michael D. Doubler. *The National Guard: An Illustrated History of America's Citizen-Soldiers*. Dulles, VA: Potomac, 2007. Print. 59–61.

5. Ibid. 66–67.

6. Michael D. Doubler. *Civilian in Peace, Soldier in War*. Lawrence, KS: UP of Kansas, 2003. Print. 186.

7. Michael D. Doubler. *The National Guard: An Illustrated History of America's Citizen-Soldiers*. Dulles, VA: Potomac, 2007. Print. 67–69.

8. Ibid. 99.

9. Michael D. Doubler. *Civilian in Peace, Soldier in War*. Lawrence, KS: UP of Kansas, 2003. Print. 237.

10. "National Guard's Deadliest Days in Vietnam." *VFW, Veterans of Foreign Wars Magazine*. VFW, Veterans of Foreign Wars, 1 May 2010. Web. 30 Mar. 2014.

11. Lt. Col. Ellen Krenke. "Army Relegates Guard to Combat Support in First Gulf War." *National Guard Bureau*. Defense Video and Imagery Distribution System, n.d. Web. 1 Apr. 2014.

12. Michael D. Doubler. *The National Guard: An Illustrated History of America's Citizen-Soldiers*. Dulles, VA: Potomac, 2007. Print. 115–116.

13. "History & Bibliography of the 'Rainbow.'" *New York State Division of Military & Naval Affairs*. New York State, n.d. Web. 30 Mar. 2014.

SOURCE NOTES CONTINUED

CHAPTER 4. AN EVOLVING ROLE IN WARTIME

1. Michael D. Doubler. *The National Guard: An Illustrated History of America's Citizen-Soldiers*. Dulles, VA: Potomac, 2007. Print. 144.
2. "ANG Heritage: Missions, Wars and Operations." *Air National Guard*. Air National Guard, n.d. Web. 30 Mar. 2014.
3. Michael D. Doubler. *The National Guard: An Illustrated History of America's Citizen-Soldiers*. Dulles, VA: Potomac, 2007. Print. 147.
4. Michael Doubler. *The National Guard and Reserve: A Reference Handbook*. Westport, CT: Praeger, 2008. Print. 137.
5. Mary Corbett. *National Guard 101: A Handbook for Spouses*. New York: Savas Beatie, 2011. Print. 13.
6. "Summary of the DOD Fiscal Year 2014 Budget Proposal." *Defense.gov*. US Department of Defense, n.d. Web. 30 Jan. 2014.
7. "FY14 Consolidated Appropriations." *National Guard Bureau Office of Legislative Liaison*. National Guard Bureau, 15 Jan. 2014. Web. 7 Apr. 2014.

CHAPTER 5. THE NATIONAL GUARD TODAY

1. "Constitution of the United States." *US Senate*. US Senate, n.d. Web. 30 Mar. 2014.
2. Michael D. Doubler. *The National Guard: An Illustrated History of America's Citizen-Soldiers*. Dulles, VA: Potomac, 2007. Print. 133.
3. Mary Corbett. *National Guard 101: A Handbook for Spouses*. New York: Savas Beatie, 2011. Print. 14.
4. Caitlin O'Neil. "Changing of the Guard: A Look Back at 10 Years of War." *Hidden Surge*. Medill National Security Journalism Initiative, 14 Feb. 2012. Web. 30 Mar. 2014.

CHAPTER 6. SERVICE AT HOME

1. Lou Dolinar. "Katrina: What the Media Missed." *Real Clear Politics*. RealClearPolitics.com, 23 May 2006. Web. 30 Mar. 2014.

2. "Army Creeds." *Washington National Guard*. Washington National Guard, n.d. Web. 1 Apr. 2014.

3. Sgt. 1st Class Jon Soucy, National Guard Bureau. "Guard's Role in Disaster Response Defined More Clearly." *US Army*. US Army, 3 Mar. 2012. Web. 30 Mar. 2014.

4. Melissa Pamer. "Los Angeles 1992 Riots: By the Numbers." *NBC Southern California*. NBCUniversal Media, 20 Apr. 2012. Web. 30 Mar. 2014.

CHAPTER 7. WEAPONS AND EQUIPMENT

1. "The United States Military Rank Insignia." *US Department of Defense*. US Department of Defense, n.d. Web. 30 Mar. 2014.

CHAPTER 8. CAREER OPPORTUNITIES

1. Chris Kenning. "National Guard Members Battle in Job Market." *USA Today*. USATODAY, 23 Oct. 2012. Web. 30 Mar. 2014.

CHAPTER 9. LIFE IN THE NATIONAL GUARD

1. Sgt. 1st Class Jim Greenhill, National Guard Bureau. "National Guard Relieves Suffering after Hurricane Sandy." *US Army*. US Army, 4 Nov. 2012. Web. 30 Mar. 2014.

INDEX

ABOUT THE AUTHOR

Marcia Amidon Lusted is the author of 90 books for young readers, as well as more than 400 magazine articles. She is an associate editor and staff writer for ePals Media/Cobblestone Publishing, as well as a writing instructor and musician. She lives in New Hampshire.